Live Foods Live Bodies · The power of Living Foods

For more information on getting permission for reprints and/or excerpts, please contact:

Kordich Group International, Inc.
PO Box 3486
Rancho Santa Fe, CA 92067

Find us on the web at:
www.jaykordich.com

Live Foods Live Bodies is a registered trademark of Kordich Group International, Inc.

ISBN 0-9770564-0-6

Printed and bound in China.
Photo credits: Edmond Fong, Cheryl Tsai, Linda Kordich, Ben Ged Low

Book Designed by: Cheryl Tsai

Jay Kordich's

A ~ Z

Juice Therapy Remedies

By Jay Kordich

Kordich House Press

"No Hurries - No Worries Be Happy"

Baldev Singh

Our friend Baldev Singh's slogan fits well in our Live Foods Live Bodies Program. Life is a journey God takes us on. All has already been written, so why not surrender to the ride of Life? Linda and I like to say -

"The Simple Life is the Best Life." Stay with simple foods, live a simple life, and you will be rewarded in ways unimaginable filled with virtue, great vital health and wisdom.

About the Author

Jay is most famous for launching the entire Juice Therapy message on TV for over 15 years. His fame brought him world-wide success. Jay has studied living foods and juicing his entire adult life, after contracting cancer in 1948. He adopted Dr. Gerson's juicing program, changing his life forever by becoming the largest advocate of juice therapy the world knows today. He has sold over two million books from his #1 New York Times best seller; *The Power of Juicing.* He is also responsible for selling close to one billion dollars of juicer sales throughout the world.

Now at the age when most people are retired and living in retirement homes, Jay, at the age of 82 boldly introduces his new multi-media program entitled: *Live Foods Live Bodies.* This is the first program of its kind to be sold around the world through retail and television.

Jay's slogan has always been:
"When you have your health, you have a future!"

Welcome

to the

World

of

Juice Therapy

Introduction

In this small but powerful booklet I am sharing with you all of the healing juice recipes I have used for the past 60 years. My mentor, Dr. Max Gerson and Dr. Norman Walker handed down some of these recipes to me to share with all who would listen and apply.

In my book *Live Foods Live Bodies* you most likely have read my life history, but in case you haven't I will briefly discuss how and why juicing is and has been so important to me.

About Jay

When I was twenty-five, playing football for the University of Southern California in 1947, I pulled a thigh muscle that threw me out of the game for an entire year. During that time, I became sick with a bladder problem that was later diagnosed as bladder cancer. I was told I had less than a year to live, or if I chose, I could go under the knife to have the tumor cut out and receive cobalt treatments. (Back in the 1940s, chemotherapy and radiation had not yet been thoroughly developed.) Cancer amongst Americans was very low in the 1940's. Unfortunately, now more than one million Americans get diagnosed per year.

I opted for another choice. I had heard of a medical doctor named Max Gerson, who was becoming an expert at healing cancer through what most people know about in Europe; juice therapy. I quickly went to visit Dr. Gerson, who at that time ran a busy cancer clinic in New York. He agreed to treat me—but only after scolding me about my eating habits and telling me how drastically I had to change my life in order to get well. I eagerly agreed, and thus began a juicing program that went on for three months, three of which were somewhat grueling. (After all, I was taught by my football coach to eat steaks, pies, cakes, and hamburgers every day.) The first three weeks on Dr. Gerson's program were almost unbearable. Yet, surprisingly, after about one week my body, mind, and soul soon took on an almost euphoric feeling. I lost weight, my skin started to clear up, I wasn't constipated any longer and I could breathe clearly. Most importantly, I wasn't bleeding in the genital area any longer. Before those three weeks, I had been bleeding every day while urinating.

After three months of Dr. Gerson's treatments, I went home and continued on my own, fasting on juices for another two years. I sipped warm broths in the winter months, and, eventually, I started adding more organic, pure foods to my diet. Even now, I consume mostly raw, unadulterated, organic fruits and vegetables. You could say that I mostly eat fruit and juice my vegetables. Why? It's very simple. Fruits are mostly water. For example, here are some fruits I recommend to eat or blend:

1. *Papaya (without skin)*
2. *Mango (without skin)*
3. *Banana (without skin)*
4. *All berries*
5. *Stone fruits (with skin)*
6. *Kiwi (with skin)*
7. *Cantaloupe (without skin)*
8. *Watermelon (without skin)*
9. *Grapes**
10. *Coconut (without shell)*
11. *Pineapple (without skin)*

*Only eat grapes with seeds-they have not been hydribidized and have more nutrients.

Below are the fruits we love to eat too, but we also recommend juicing these fruits too.

Apples with skin
Pineapple (without the peel)
Pears (extra firm-if soft, we eat them)
Oranges (without skin)
All melons (with skins only if organic)
Grapefruit (without peel)

Apples are not good blended, yet pineapples, pears and oranges blend well, but we prefer to eat these fruits because they have less water content than the others and they are rich with fiber, as our bodies need large amounts of daily in order to function at its optimum.

The cancer scare in the 1940s started me on a mission to teach others about the healing power of juice therapy. I gave up my studies at USC, unfortunately only a few credits short of receiving my bachelors of science degree. Obviously I gave up a rich football career and lifestyle for this commitment, and I'm so grateful I did. I have spent the last fifty-seven years traveling across North America extolling the virtues of juicing, and my life is richer than before, blessed with health, vitality, and happiness even now in the year 2005. Even though I lost my precious trademark and ability to teach for ten years, I still consider myself blessed with wonderful, vital health everyday.

When you don't have your health, it doesn't matter how rich, happy, or successful you are. Illness has a way of stopping everything in its tracks.

It's personally heartbreaking to see people purchase juicers and end up using them occasionally for fruit juicing and smoothies for fun at parties. Juicing is a very serious subject, one that I have spent my entire life dedicated to, and, ultimately, teaching. Since l993, I have not been able to publish books on juicing, due to trademark challenges; otherwise, I would have written many more juicing books. Since I have decided to move onward without using this trademarked name, Linda and I have decided to borrow from our life savings, publish our own line of books, making access to my teaching available directly to you, through our Web site and infomercial.

> *Anyone can sell you a juicer, but my mission in life is to teach these natural, universal truths—truths that will literally change your life and help you heal!*

Good luck and remember to apply what you learn and share it with others as you go through life.

Jay Kordich
- The Father of Juicing.

Know Your Phytochemicals!

Plants have developed their own protective substances called phytochemicals from the word "phyton" the greek term for plant. Mounting research shows that many phytochemicals also protect humans against cancer and other degenerative diseases. Note, that when these phytochemicals are in juice form, they are more concentrated and have the ability to heal and regenerate faster and more efficiently, as the juices go into the bloodstream immediately. As you read under 'FUNCTION' you will see that almost every answer for function deals with enzymes, a subject which I cannot stress enough that we desperate need in our diets to maintain a healthy body.

PHYTOCHEMICALS	FUNCTION	SOURCES
Allylic sulfides	may stimulate production Of productive enzymes	Garlic, onions
Bioflavinoids	Antioxidant, inhibits cancer Promoting hormones	most fresh fruits and veggies
Catechins (Tannins)	Protects against Tobacco induced carcinogens	Berries, green tea
Catechins	Antioxdant	All berries, green tea
Genistein	Inhibits tumor growth	Broccoli and other Cruciferous Veggies
Indols	Inhibits estrogens that Stimulates some cancers; Induces protective enzymes	Broccoli, cabbage, mustard greens, cauliflower

Isoflavones	inhibits estrogen uptake Destroys cancer enzymes	Beans, peanuts & other legumes
Isothiocyanates	Induces production of Protective enzymes	Horseradish, mustard radishes
Lignans	Inhibits estrogen and Blocks prostaglandins	Flax seeds, walnuts
Limonoids	Induces protective enzymes	All citrus fruits
Lycopene	Anti-oxidant, may protect against prostate cancer	Tomatoes, pink grapefruit, watermelon
Monoterpenes	Some anti-oxidant properties Aids in activity of protective Enzymes	Basil, Broccoli, citrus fruits, orange and yellow vegetables

Omega-3 Fatty Acids	Inhibits estrogen and reduces inflammation	Flax seeds, walnuts spinach
Phenolic Acid	Inhibits nitrosamines Enhances enzyme activity	Berries, broccoli, citrus fruits, carrots,Eggplants, parsley, peppers, teas, tomato, whole grains
Protease	Destroys enzyme inhibitors That promote cancer spread	Soy beans
Quercitin	Inhibits cellular mutation Carcinogens, clot formations And inflammation	Grape skins
Terpenes	Stimulates anti-cancer enzymes	Citrus Fruits

Know Your Vegetables:

Most of us, here in America know we should be eating more and more vegetables everyday, but truthfully we really don't have a relationship with vegetables. Most of us know what potatoes, corn and tomatoes are because we consistently eat them. However, foods like Cauliflower, Brussels Sprouts, Asparagus, and grains such as Barley and Quinoa. This small chapter is designed to introduce a small number of these special Fruits, vegetables and grains to help open your world up just a bit. Linda and I give you a basic understanding of how these foods can help heal your body, and then some personal experiences with these foods that can be either applied towards juicing combinations of just basic information that is good to know. Take it from the experts like Linda and me. We have used these foods, all in different ways, over and over again.

Once you familiarize yourself with these foods, your creative juices will start to flow, whereby you will become better at preparing natural foods in just a short period of time. As Linda and I like to say, welcome to our World of Living Foods –so here we go!

Here are some foods we recommend for your own LIVING KITCHEN PANTRY:

Apple
Reduces cholesterol, contains cancer-fighting agent known as antioxidant. High in fiber, helps prevent constipation and suppresses appetite. A great staple for all vegetable and fruit juice recipes. Jay and I recommend Fuji apples for eating, red and golden delicious for juicing, and granny smith and pippin for juicing when you want more of a tart taste. Pippins are great for our Living Pies.

Asparagus
A super source of glutathione, a powerful antioxidant. In studies, glutathione has been shown to act against at least thirty carcinogens. We recommend juicing Asparagus with Kale and Carrots in 33% increments, meaning they are all equal.

Avocado
Can help prevent clogging of arteries; dilates blood vessels. Lowers cholesterol. Its main fat, monounsaturated oleic acid, acts as an antioxidant, slowing the buildup LDL (low-density lipoprotein) cholesterol. Also one of the richest sources of glutathione. We love avocados here in California and recommend Haas Avocados or

Bacon avocados. Make sure when you purchase avocados that they are not too soft, for if they are, they will be browned and smell 'off' when opened. Best to buy firm, but just a bit soft to the touch. We love avocados in sandwiches, salsas, living soups and salads.

Banana

Soothes the stomach. Strengthens the stomach lining against acid and ulcers, and lab tests show that bananas can act like antibiotics. Very high in potassium, thus may help regulate high blood pressure. Bananas are the staple in most all smoothies. If you can not tolerate bananas, we recommend young baby coconuts natural mineral water and white soft meat as a substitute for smoothies. We always try to buy bananas organically because they come from different sources from around the world, and if they are not organic, then we worry–and for good reason. Foreign countries do not have standards any where near to ours, and when the produce comes in from their country, USDA only spot checks their produce, and for us, that's just not acceptable. Bananas are also our biggest staple in our super green smoothies.

Barley

Long considered a heart medicine in the Middle East. Reduces cholesterol levels and contains antioxidants that may help prevent cancer. We love Barley, and also use the Pearl Barley form, which is basically just polished Barley. Remember to always soak your grains for a few hours (at least, before you cook them).

Beans

(including navy, black, kidney, and pinto beans, and lentils) Studies show that eating a half cup of cooked beans daily may reduce cholesterol levels as much as 10 percent. Also helps to regulate blood-sugar levels. Very high in fiber. Bean consumption is linked to lower rates of prostate and breast cancer. We do not eat too many beans, as they are harder to digest than most of all the other foods we consume in our Live Foods Live Bodies Program. However, when you soak your beans overnight before you cook them, it aids in better digestion, no doubt. We recommend eating beans with a dominant (living foods) salad to help digest them even better.

Bell Pepper

Super-rich in antioxidant vitamin C. Therefore, a great food for fighting off colds, asthma, bronchitis, respiratory infections and cataracts, as well as angina, atherosclerosis (damaged, clogged arteries) and cancer. Jay and I are not fond of Green bell peppers. We are however, fond of red, yellow and orange bell peppers. The taste is sweeter and the red bell pepper is actually a more riper version of the green bell pepper.

Blueberries

Acts as an unusual type of antibiotic by keeping infectious bacteria from attaching to the lining of the urinary tract, helping to prevent recurring urinary tract and bladder infections. Also contain chemicals that curb diarrhea. We love blueberries, and sometimes fantasize about living in Seattle, Washington whereby they grow wild! Getting more down to earth, we realize that only a few times per year are they in season, and when they are, we love to eating them in fruit salads, in smoothies (primarily) and in our Living Pies. Please buy berries organically. Berries are full of pesticides–sometimes containing more than fifteen different sprays.

Broccoli & Cauliflower

Abundant in antioxidants. Broccoli is rich in anticancer agent such as vitamin C, beta carotene and quercetin. Both broccoli and cauliflower are considered effective in helping to prevent lung, colon, and breast cancers. These cruciferous vegetables can speed up removal of estrogen from the body, perhaps helping to prevent hormone–related cancers such as breast cancer. Rich in fiber. Compounds in broccoli also help prevent ulcers. We love broccoli and cauliflower because not only do we love them in juice form combined with carrots and parsley, we love them in salads, chopped and diced, and we love them in their raw form as crudités, and finally steamed with organic brown rice.

Brussels Sprouts

Possess some of the same powers as their cruciferous cousins broccoli and cabbage. Packed with antioxidants and other cancer-fighters including indoles, chemicals that may help protect against colon cancer. Remember, brussels sprouts

Combined with green beans produce a natural amount of insulin and is great for diabetics. See our juicing chapter in our book Live Foods Live Bodies for the recipe. I personally love Brussels sprouts, diced or sliced very thinly in our vegetable salads. They go great with pumpkin seeds in our salads too.

Cabbage

Contains numerous anti-cancer and antioxidant compounds. Seems to suppress the growth of colon polyps, a precursor to colon cancer; in studies, eating cabbage more than once a week cut men's colon cancer odds by 66 percent. Further, studies conducted by Dr. Garnet Chaney have found that pure cabbage juice, and sometimes combined with carrots and celery actually cure stomach ulcers, duodenal and peptic. We love cabbage juice, and interestingly taste very sweet as juice.

Carrot

A super source of beta carotene, the antioxidant reputed to help prevent numerous health problems, including heart attacks, cancer, and cataracts. One study showed that the beta carotene in a daily cup of carrots slashed stroke rates in women by 40 percent and heart attacks by 22 percent. One medium carrot's worth of beta carotene daily may cut lung-cancer risk in half, even among formerly heavy smokers. Did you know that carrot juice is almost identical to the structure to our human blood? Carrot juice, as you most likely know by now, is our biggest staple in our Living Kitchen, used not only in salads but in juice form, as the dominant player. Shredded, diced, chopped, steamed, juiced – it's all there with our star – carrots!

Celery

Celery compounds have been shown to lower blood pressure in animals. High in certain anticancer compounds that have been shown to detoxify carcinogens, including cigarette smoke. tests also show celery may act as a mild diuretic. We love celery because it helps us lose weight because of its natural diuretic capabilities, but it's also great as a basic ingredient in our Pate's and in most of our Digestive Juice Aids.

Chili Pepper

Revs up the blood clot-dissolving system, opens sinuses and air passages, and acts as a decongestant. Most of its pharmacological activity is credited to capsaicin, the compound that makes the pepper taste hot. Capsaicin is also a potent painkiller, alleviating headaches when inhaled. Putting hot chili sauce on food may even speed up metabolism, burning off calories. We highly recommend juicing chili's with any of our Digestive Juice Aids to create 'heat' and help stimulate the blood vessels. We love chili's in salsas and pate's. Definitely a must have in our Living Kitchen, and remember, there are so many different kinds. We recommend Anaheim chili peppers if you don't like them too hot. Then there's the die hards who love the 'heat'. For them we recommend Jalapeno peppers with the seeds!

Cinnamon

A strong stimulator of insulin activity; thus, potentially helpful for those with adult-onset diabetes. Also seems to help prevent blood clots. We recommend only organic cinnamon and we use cinnamon a lot as an addition to our fruit smoothies and as a topping at the last minute on our Living Pies.

Clove
Long used to dull the pain of toothache. Contains compounds that act like aspirin. Cloves are very strong, but we use them organically, ground up in our smoothies and Living Pies.

Collard Greens
Full of antioxidant compounds, including lutein, vitamin C and beta carotene. In animal studies, collards inhibited the spread of breast cancer. Collard-green consumption, like that of other green leafy vegetables, is associated with low rates of many cancers. As you may know by now, please make sure to juice bitter greens such as Collard Greens in a 33% dilution of carrot/collard greens/apple or beet. This way the bitterness is eased, and it goes down easier and most likely you will be juicing this green more and more. And we hope you do, as it's one of the most powerfully rich greens you can eat.

Corn
High in anticancer compounds called protease inhibitors, corn may help fight cancer and act as an antiviral agent. We show corn here just because it's so good in its RAW form over salads, tostadas, and wraps. However we don't recommend eating

corn unless it's in season during the summertime, and not in fresh juice form either.

Cranberries

Like blueberries, help prevent recurring urinary tract and bladder infections. Also believed to be effective in inhibiting viruses. One of Jay's absolute favorite berries. Cranberries, naturally in season during late October through December, we recommend cranberries in smoothies, juices and dried over salads. This is a powerful food, such as the Pomegranate, with capabilities yet to be discovered by scientists. Some older Doctor friends' of Jay tell him that Pomegranate and Cranberries can actually dissolve benign tumors. Dates. High in natural aspirin. Also high in fiber; have a laxative effect. Dried fruits, including dates, are linked to lower rates of certain cancers, especially pancreatic cancer.

Garlic

A proven antibiotic that has been shown to kill bacteria, fungi, and intestinal parasites. Also shown to lower blood-cholesterol levels, seems to act as an anticoagulant. Garlic also contains multiple anticancer compounds, antioxidants, and immune-system boosters. A good cold medication, garlic also acts as an effective decongestant and anti-inflammatory agent. What would we do without Garlic? We use it in

everything; salads, soups, living soups, acceptable cooked foods, and fresh vegetable juices.
Pick garlic that is firm, white and not mildewed in any form, and please buy organic.

Ginger

Used for centuries in Asia, ginger is a proven anti-nausea remedy. Also, relieves the inflammatory pain and swelling of rheumatoid arthritis and osteoarthritis. We adore ginger because it can really pop in flavor when it comes to smoothies, fruit juice blends, salads and salad dressings. Most people don't know that ginger is a root, and you need to purchase ginger when it's pink in color or yellow. Never gray or bluish in color, as that would mean it's full of fungus, old and not edible. When you juice ginger, you don't have to peel it to juice, but when you use it in dressings or in other things such as smoothies, you need to peel the skin off.

Grapefruit

Contains a pectin that's been shown to lower blood-cholesterol levels and blood pressure in animals. High in antioxidants, especially disease-fighting vitamin C, grapefruit may help prevent stomach and pancreatic cancer. Grapefruit/Pineapple is one of Jay's favorite blends. 50/50. Just make sure to peel the grapefruit's skin off completely, as the oils are flammable, and also please remember to leave as much of the 'pith' white skin as possible on the grapefruit, as it's very high in bio-flavinoids, (high in vitamin C). We recommend Red Grapefruit and Pink Grapefruit for juice. Look for soft grapefruits, whereby their skin is shiny and their pores very small. Watch out for big pores in the skin, as that will tell you they are not ripe.

Grapes

A rich storehouse of anti-cancer compounds, red grapes are high in the antioxidant quercetin. Red-grade skins also contain resveratrol, which seems to lower bad-type LDL cholesterol. One of Jay's favorite fruits are grapes. Try reading the book, (that is, if it's still in print); The Grape Cure by Johanna Brandt. Grapes are totally underrated, but Jay has been eating and juicing grapes for years, trust me–I know because I have purchased grapes for 25 years! His favorite grapes are: Concord grapes (they only come out once a year, but are worth the wait). Also he recommend grapes with SEEDS only. Red grapes with seeds are his second favorite. Please try to purchase grapes that are organic only, because like berries grapes are full of pesticides, and some say up to 33 different kinds of sprays are used.

Kale

An amazingly rich source of antioxidant

compounds. High in beta carotene, and contains more lutein than any other vegetable tested. Kale is a member of the cruciferous family and contains anticancer chemicals called indoles, which may help prevent estrogen-linked cancers. Kale is a wonderful green, and almost a super-green because of it's superior antioxidant properties. We recommend juicing kale with carrots, parsley and/or apples. Kale is also good in salads, but Kale needs to soak first for awhile because it's tough to eat, but when it is soaked for about an hour, it will soften up and be easier to eat in salad form. Look for deep rich colors of green, whereby the leaves are not wilty, nor full of holes from critters.

Melon
(cantaloupe and honeydew) May help prevent blood clots. Orange melons, such as cantaloupe, also contain high levels of beta carotene. Melons alone or leave them alone is the cure here. Always eat your fruit salads without melons. Watermelon is one of Jay's favorite kidney cleansers, and Jay believes that in time, Scientists will find that Watermelons are greater for us than previously believed.

Mushroom
Esteemed in Asia as a heart medicine and cancer preventive. Tests show that compounds in Asian

mushrooms, such as shiitake, may help inhibit cancer as well as viral diseases, and can lower cholesterol levels. One study showed that fresh or dried shiitake mushrooms cut cholesterol by up to 12 percent when eaten daily. As you most likely can see, we are not much on mushrooms, however they are a wonderful substitute for meat in soup bases and in veggie-burger recipes. We do not eat them in salads, and recommend, believe it or not, in cooked form. They are a fungus, so therefore we recommend them to be cooked, as we don't want to put any foreign bacteria in our bodies that may disrupt our ecosystem. We recommend button mushrooms and shitake mushrooms. Make sure they are connected to the stem and that they are free of fungus.

Nuts

High in the antioxidant vitamin E., nuts help prevent cancer and heart disease. Almonds have a high concentration of oleic acid, which may help reduce cholesterol and protect arteries. Brazil nuts are extremely rich in selenium, an antioxidant linked to lower rates of both heart disease and cancer. And walnuts contain ellagic acid, another cholesterol-reducer. Recent studies show peanuts gaining a lot of respect when it comes to reducing cholesterol. We do NOT recommend any kind of nut to be purchased in roasted form, nor heated in any way. This automatically creates the oils, which are good for us to turn rancid and can actually hurt our arteries. Buy only fresh, organic nuts, and preferably refrigerated to keep down possible fungus growth, which happens regularly with nuts.

Oats
Oats can help lower cholesterol and stabilize blood-sugar levels. Compounds in oats also seem to suppress nicotine cravings. Did you know oats as we mostly know them are really a groat? They are hard in form and almost impossible to eat in oatmeal form as we know them, because through processing they are flattened and shaved so we can eat them easily in breakfast cereals. We love oats and even the steel cut oats are great either in muesli or regular oatmeal form. Purchase organically and in bulk form is ok as long as they look fresh.

Onion
Including chives, shallots, scallions, leeks) Containing exceptionally strong antioxidants, onions have been shown to help prevent cancer in animals. The onion is a rich source of quercetin, a potent antioxidant known to inhibit stomach cancer. Onions may also help prevent atherosclerosis and blood clots, and even high fight bacterial and viral infections. Because the body sees cooked foods as foreign, it attacks

the cooked foods. This is the reason why we recommend onions of any kind placed over your cooked meal. We love onions and our favorites are the maui sweet onion. Whenever buying onions please remember to purchase them as hard as possible without any graying or bluish spots on them. They should be firm and in tact without all their dried onion skins in disarray.

Orange

A complete package of cancer-inhibitors, including antioxidants such as vitamin C. Specifically tied to lower rates of pancreatic cancer. Because of their high vitamin C content, oranges may also help ward off breast and stomach cancer, asthma attacks, atherosclerosis, and gum disease. Some studies show that vitamin C deficiencies may also inhibit fertility in some men. We love oranges and use them in smoothies and in juice form quite frequently. We only recommend organic of course, but we love navels for eating, and Valencia oranges for juicing, as they have the most juice. Gently peel the skin, leaving as much of the white skin as possible onto the orange before you either juice or blend it. Small pored oranges are usually full of more juice than larger pored oranges.

Parsley

Rich in antioxidants, parsley can help detoxify carcinogens, including those in tobacco smoke.

Parsley also acts as a diuretic.
If you have a tooth infection, Jay recommends a parsley poultice/onion poultice. The parsley and onions are diced in very fine form, then wrapped into the cheesecloth and then placed onto the infected part of the mouth or sore. It actually draws out the infection. Parsley is not a vegetable, rather it's an herb. There are currently two popular forms of parsley, one is flat leaf (Italian) and original. Jay prefers the original form, as he believes it has more medicinal values. We use parsley in many of our Digestive Juice Aids and consider it to be one of top 5 in powerhouse capabilities for greens.

Plum and Prune

Compounds in these fruits may act as antibacterial and antiviral agents. High in fiber, these fruits work as laxatives. Always try to buy organic prunes and make sure that there is NO sulphur dioxide in the prunes or plums (if they are dried), because in most cases this is true. However in more enlightened health food grocery stores you will find organic and sulphur free dried fruits such as prunes and plums.

Pumpkin

Extremely high in beta carotene. We love pumpkin and use it in soups during the fall time, however it does not juice well, so we try to keep in line with this fact, and try to consume pumpkins in soup form, and in steamed form. Best to purchase pumpkins that are firm, not having any soft spots on them.

Raspberries

As do other berries, raspberries help fight infections, and may help prevent some cancers. Also help curb nausea. All berries in our opinion are highly underrated and we now are finding out they are they lowest in 'glycemic' sugars of all the fruits, and the highest in anti-oxidants of most all the fruits. Their pigmented colors (bright colors) are the best of all fruits, thereby giving us the highest forms of anti-oxidants and protective factors for keeping our pancreas balanced. We love berries and try to buy them as often as possible, but for sure only organically.

Rice

(white and brown) Like other seeds, contains anticancer protease inhibitors. Effective against diarrhea. Rice bran helps lower cholesterol levels and may help prevent formation of kidney stones.

We all need carbohydrates in our diet, otherwise our brains will shrivel up and die! We however only recommend either organic short grain brown rice, long grain brown rice and regular California brown rice, not basmati or white or sticky rice.

These rices are simple carbohydrates, whereby the body sees them as sugars, whereas brown rice are complex, therefore the sugars slowly get into the bloodstream, helping the pancreas process the foods in better balance. Always look for organic and in bins whereby the rice is free of fungus and/or small rocks. Purchasing rice already packaged is our best choice.

Soybeans

(tofu) Rich in compounds that act like hormones and thus seem to ward off cancer, especially estrogen-linked breast cancer. High soybean consumption may be one reason rates of breast cancer and prostate cancers are very low among the Japanese. In studies, soybeans lowered blood cholesterol levels substantially. And animal studies showed that soybeans seem to deter and help dissolve kidney stones. We love TOFU! Tofu comes in so many different forms. First let us say that we highly recommend organic tofu, because somehow Americans have found a way to create a cheaper soybean, whereby they genetically modify them, which in our natural world is a big no no. This is why we recommend only organic tofu. There are many kinds of tofu: soft (in aseptic boxes), which we do not recommend, as it just doesn't taste good, nor does it taste fresh. So we recommend soft, medium, firm and extra firm. Soft for soups and smoothies, medium for stir frys (without oils) and firm and extra firm for salads. Try buying the Japanese kind of tofu in the refrigerated section of your grocery store, and remember organic!

Spinach

As with other green leafy vegetables, consumption of spinach is linked with lower rates of cancer. A super source of antioxidants, including folate, beta carotene and lutein, for example. Jay and I don't believe Spinach has received it's deserving rewards...it's an underrated vegetable with stellar capabilities for healing digestive problems. In our Digestive Juice Aids we use spinach exclusively in every recipe as it's the KING of digestion and healer of almost all stomach lesions. We like to buy baby spinach for our salads, and regular adult spinach for our juices. Spinach is great in all salads, vegetable juice combinations such as carrot/spinach/celery/beet and apple. We do not recommend cooking spinach, ever. Cooked spinach is a completely different food when it's cooked, creating not only oxalic acid in larger forms, but all of its healing properties die when cooked.

Strawberries

Rich in antioxidant vitamin C as well as high in fiber. Studies show that compounds in strawberries act like antiviral agents. And other studies link regular strawberry consumption to lower rates of all types of cancer. Try to only buy strawberries in organic form, and only in season.

Sweet Potato

A blockbuster source of beta carotene. One half-cup of mashed sweet potatoes is higher in beta carotene than a medium carrot. Also high in fiber. Sweet Potatoes are not good in juice form, but are great steamed and put into salads to make them a whole meal salad. We love cooked sweet potatoes in the wintertime in soups-indeed they are a food few of us eat, yet are sweet, filling and delicious. Purchase firm, with no soft spots and the with the least amount of scars and dark spots. They will last a few weeks once you bring them home, but make sure they do not start to sprout.

Tea

(including black, oolong, and green tea) Tea acts as an antibactial, anti-ulcer agent, cavity-fighter, even an anti-diarrheal agent. In animal studies, tea and tea compounds seemed to inhibit various cancers. Tea drinkers appear to have lower risk of atherosclerosis and stroke. Perhaps that's because they are not coffee drinkers! Jay and I vehemently do not recommend coffee whatsoever. However, teas are highly recommended. Sometimes in the summertime, you can brew an herbal tea, and mix it with fruit juice combinations of your choice, then add ice. We highly recommend only organic teas.

Tomato

A major source of the antioxidant lycopene. tomatoes are linked to low rates of certain cancers, including bladder cancer. We only recommend raw tomatoes, and we use them in salads, green smoothies and vegetable juice combinations. Tomatoes are a fruit, believe it or not, but they are wonderful foods, and we love the new heirloom varieties, and the vine ripened deep red tomatoes in the summertime. Purchase soft but firm, never with bruises or 'off' in smell.

Watermelon

Like the tomato, watermelon contains high levels of lycopene and glutathione, an antioxidant and anticancer compounds. One of our favorite fruits, Watermelon is a grand experience, and probably one of the king's of fruits. High in water content, it's a fantastic kidney cleanser and diuretic. It's also very high in natural mineral water.

Know your Juice Therapy Combinations

Since I have been teaching juice therapy to millions of Americans for close to sixty years, I will tell you that this particular teaching can have the most profound potential healing ability, and in fact, can completely turn the body around to better health in just days. Most importantly, it brings the body around in the way of alkalizing it with the liquid juices. Secondly, it is full of natural minerals, assimilated easily through the juice form, Including living enzymes and vitamins. Correct juice combing, on a regular basis can literally change your life, the way it did for me.

First, let's talk a bit about minerals. The most important minerals for the body are: Iron, Iodine, Calcium and Phosphorous, unfortunately these elements are frequently lacking in the average American diet. The blood cells must be adequately supplied with iron in order to build new red blood cells; without iodine, the thyroid gland cannot form thyroxine, goitrous conditions and related glandular disturbances are the result;

without phosphorus the body cannot utilize calcium and without calcium the whole skeletal system is weakened, the teeth, nails, skin and hair all suffer.

Mineral Starvation means slow death to all of the beautiful and intricate mechanisms of the body. Happily we have, in fruit and vegetables juices, the means of supplying the body with all the essential minerals and vitamins in easily digested and quickly assimilable form, plus a generous supply of chlorophyll.

All green juices have a plethora of chlorophyll. Liquid, living greens have no substitute, and are filled with natural minerals. It is not only the mineral and vitamin content of fruit and vegetable juices that makes their use so beneficial, it is also due to the presence of various organic compounds, of highly complex chemical structures, that exists as vegetable amino-acids; as compounds functioning similarly to some of the body secretions, juices and hormones. Juices, we find natural organic compounds, which when extracted and crystallized, have long been recognized as important aids in the armory of therapies.

INCOMPATIBILITIES
A few of the fruit and veggie juices are NOT compatible and should not be combined together:

- **Apricot with greens/veggies**
- **Blackberry with greens/veggies**
- **Figs with greens/veggies**
- **Grapes with carrots**
- **Grapefruits with greens/veggies**
- **Lemons/limes with veggies**
- **Orange with veggies/greens**

COMPATIBLES

Apples are compatible w/all fruits and vegetables
Carrot compatible w/all veggies.
Prune Use only blended, compatible with all fruits, including fennel

Fruit and vegetable juices are not medicines, they are protective corrective and supplementary foods that supply the body with bio-genic, 100% assimilable nutrients containing great supplies of minerals, vitamins, and enzymes, phyto-nutrients and antioxidants, including the yet unidentified nutrients science has yet to discover.
Before you decide to juice or take any kind of

a fast, please consult your family physician.

A–Z AILMENTS

Here is our list of common ailments that we believe will respond favorably to raw juice therapy. Remember our aim is to cleanse the bloodstream allowing the body to relieve the cause of these un natural disorders.

These juices will help build up your immune system. You should be drinking 4–8, 8 ounce glasses per day. Each one of our remedies are designed to bring about 16 ounces.

1. Acidosis
10 Carrots/handful of spinach/2 ribs celery/1/4 green cabbage

2. Acne
10 Carrots/handfull of spinach/2 ribs celery/1/2 cup watercress

3. Adenoids
10   Carrots/handful of spinach

4. Allergies
10 carrots/handful of spinach and/or 10 carrots/1/4 beet/1 cucumber, peeled

5. Anemia
10 carrots/handful of spinach/2 ribs celery/ handful of parsley/1/2 beet and/or
10 carrots/1/2 fennel and/or
1/2 pomegranate (with skin) and/or one coconut mineral water and its pulp. (blend)

6. Appendicitis
4 ribs celery/12 carrots/ and/or
10 carrots/1 cucumber and/or
10 carrots/1 rib celery/handful of parsley/ handful of spinach

7. Appetite Loss
Handful of dandelion greens /3 ribs celery/1/2 turnip/3 red radishes

8. Arthritis
3 ribs celery/1 cucumber/10 carrots/1/2 cup

endive/1 golden delicious apple

9. Asthma
10 Carrots/2 cloves garlic/ and/or
10 carrots/handful of spinach/1/2 cup
endive

10. Immune Deficient
3 ribs celery/1/2 green cabbage/large
handful of spinach/1 clove garlic/1 green
apple

11. Gallbladder
2 ribs celery/1 green apple/1 vine ripened
tomato/10 carrots/handful of spinach/1/2
lemon without the peel. (an exception to
the rule–gallbladder needs the lemon in this
combination).

12. Bladder
10 carrots/1/2 beet with greens/1 cucumber
without peel and/or
10 Carrots /handful of spinach and/or 2
green Apples/1/2 beet with its greens.

13. Boils
10 carrots/handful of spinach/1 clove garlic/

handful of parsley

14. Body Cleanser
10 Carrots/1/2 cup cabbage/2 ribs celery/1/2 cup dandelion greens/2 golden delicious apples

15. Bone builder
Handful of spinach/1/2 turnip/handful of watercress/10 carrots

16. Bronchitis
12 Carrots/2 cloves garlic/1 inch horseradish root.

17. Cancers
12 Carrots/large handful of spinach and/or 12 carrots/large handful of spinach/handful of parsley/1 green apple/1/4 beet with greens

18. Cataracts
10 Carrots/handful of watercress/handful of spinach

19. Cirrhosis of the Liver
12 Carrots/large handful of spinach and/or 3 apples/1/2 beet with its greens and/or 10 carrots/1/2 beet with its greens /1 cucumber

peeled unless organic

20. Colds
10 Carrots/2 cloves garlic/1/2 inch horseradish/2 golden apples/handful of parsley and/or
3 Apples/1/2 inch horseradish (you can dilute with water) and/or
hot water with fresh lemon juice and honey

21. Colitis
12 Carrots/large handful of spinach and/or
1 whole coconut pulp and its mineral water /2 pears, firm.

22. Conjunctivitis
10 Carrots/2 large endive leaves/handful of parsley/2 ribs celery

23. Constipation
4 Fresh figs/2 apples/1 rib of rhubarb.
Juice the apples and rhubarb. Place into a blender and blend with figs.
10 Carrots/handful of spinach

24. Coughs
10 Carrots/handful of spinach/1 inch horseradish

25. Cramps(mentrual or other)
14 Carrots/2 ribs celery

26. Cystitis
10 Carrots/2 ribs celery/1 cucumber, peeled unless organic

27. Diabetes
10 Carrots/1/4 head lettuce/5 brussel sprouts/6-8 string beans

28. Diarrhea
12 Carrots/large handful of spinach and/or 1/2 cup fresh cranberries/3 golden apples

29. Duodenal & Peptic Ulcers
1/2 Green cabbage/12 carrots

30. Eczema
10 Carrots/1 cucumber, peeled unless organic

31. Epilepsy
12 Turnip and leaves/handful of watercress/ handful of spinach

32. Fatigue
10 Carrots/handful of spinach and/or
10 Carrots/1/2 beet with greens/
1/2cucumber without peel unless organic

33. Fever
3 inch slice Watermelon with its rind unless
it's not organic and/or
12 Carrots/1 cucumber without peel unless
organic/1/2 red bell pepper.

34. Flatulence (gas)
10 Carrots/2 ribs celery/handful of each,
parsley and spinach

35. Gallbladder (congested)
Handful of dandelion leaves/2 leaves of
endive/1 vine ripened tomato/10 carrots

36. Gallstones
4 Green apples/1/2 beet and/or
1 large grapefruit without the peel/1/4 cup
olive oil/2 cloves garlic/2 oranges, peeled,
but leave as much white pulp as possible.

37. Gastric problems
4 golden apples/2 firm pears

38. Goiter
Large handful of spinach/12 carrots and/or 1/2 head lettuce/handful watercress and 10 carrots

39. Gout
5 Celery/1 cucumber, peeled, unless organic and/or 10 carrots/handful of spinach

40. Hallitosis (bad breath)
10 Carrots/handful of each: spinach and parsley

41. Hay Fever
10 Carrots/2 ribs celery/handful of parsley/1 clove garlic

42. Heart troubles
10 Carrots/2 ribs celery/1/2 cucumber, peeled unless it's organic/1/4 head green cabbage/handful of spinach

43.Headaches
4 Golden Delicious Apples/4 stalks of celery

44.Hyperacidity
12 Carrots/ 1/2 head green cabbage, cut in slices to fit throught the juicer

45.Hypertension(high blood pressure)
10 Carrots/2 cloves garlic/large handful of parsley/1 rib celery/1/4 cup dandelion/large handful of spinach and/or
10 Carrots/handful of spinach and/or
10 Carrots/1/2 beet with greens/ 1/2 cucumber, peeled unless organic

46.Hypoadrenia (Adrenal Deficiency)
10 Carrots/handful of spinach and/or 1/2 peeled pineapple and/or
3 inch slice watermelon

47. Impotence
Handful of Watercress and spinach, each/
12 Carrots

48. Immune System
12 Carrots/1/2 yam/1 inch fresh ginger/1 clove garlic/2 golden apples

49. Indigestion
12 Carrots/handful of spinach and/or
1 Lemon without peel /2 golden apples

50. Infections
12 Carrots/2 cloves garlic/handful parsley/1
large vine ripened tomato/handful of
spinach

51. Insomnia
3 golden Apples/4 ribs celery/1/2 head
lettuce

52. Jaundice
10 Carrots/handful of spinach/handful of
dandelion leaves/2 golden apples and/or 2
cups dark, seeded black grapes

53. Kidney and Bladder troubles
3 Cucumbers, peeled unless organic/10
carrots/handful of parsley/handful of
dandelion greens
And/or 3–5 inch slice of watermelon, and its
rind unless it's not organic.

54. Laryngitis
1/2 Pineapple with skin unless it's not organic and/or
1/2 anise root with 3 golden delicious apples

55. Liver (congested)
10 Carrots/1/2 beet with its greens/1 cucumber, peeled unless organic and/or 5 green apples/1 beet with its greens and/or 10 carrots/handful of spinach/2 cloves garlic

56. Low Blood Pressure
1/2 Beet with greens/2 golden apples and/or grape (dark) grapes with seeds and/or 1/2 whole pomegranate/3 green apples

57. Menstrual Disorders
10 Carrots/handful of spinach/2 ribs celery and/or 1/2 Pineapple and/or
1/2 cup blackberry/2 green apples

58. Menopause
10 Carrots/large handful of spinach and/or 10 carrots 1/2/beet with greens/1 cup

romaine lettuce/1/2 turnip and/or 1/2 pomegranate and/or
10 carrots 1/2 /beet with greens
/1 cucumber with peel unless organic

59. Nervous Disorders
10 Carrots/4 ribs celery/1/2 cup lettuce/1 clove garlic and/or
5 Apples and/or
1 cup seeded grapes (dark in color)/2 green apples and/or
10 Carrots/3 ribs celery/handful of spinach/3 endive leaves.

60. Obesity
12 Carrots/handful of spinach/2 ribs celery/1/2 cup lettuce and/or
1/2 Lemon with peel, unless it's not organic
1/grapefruit with NO peel.

61. Pleurisy
10 Carrots/1 cucumber with peel unless it's not organic/handful of spinach

62. Pimples
10 Carrots/1 cucumber with peel unless it's not organic and/or

2 Grapefuits without peel and/or
1 cup Black, or dark seeded grapes
with two golden apples.

63. Pneumonia
12 Carrots/handful of spinach and/or
1 inch Horseradish/2 apples/1/2 lemon with
peel and/or
12 Carrots/2 radishes/large handful of
spinach

64. Prostate Trouble
12 Carrots/3 radishes/1 head romaine
lettuce and/or
12 Carrots/handful of spinach and/or 12
carrots/1/2 beet with greens, if it's organic
/1 cucumber with peel, organic.

65. Psoriasis
12 Carrots/handful of spinach and/or
2 cups fresh cranberries and 2 golden
apples

66. Pyorrhea (gum disease)
Large handful of spinach/12 carrots/
1 cucumber, peeled unless it's organic

67. Rheumatism
12 Carrots/2 ribs celery/1 cucumber with peel unless it's not organic and/or
5 Apples/1 lemon with peel

68. Sciatica
2 ribs Celery/2 cucumbers, peeled, unless it's organic /10 carrots/handful of spinach

69. Scurvy
1 Grapefruit, without peel/1 lemon with peel/2 oranges and/or
1 cup Cranberry/1 large grapefruit without peel

70. Sinusitis
12 Carrots/2 large leaves endive/1 large vine ripened tomato/handful of parsley/1/4 onion/2 cloves garlic/1/4 inch horseradish

71. Sore throat
1/2 Pineapple without the skin, unless it's organic and/or
1 cup Cranberries/1 lemon with peel/1 inch ginger/2 golden apples

72. Spleen disorders
1 cup Dandelion/14 carrots/1/2 cup watercress

73. Stomach ulcers
1/2 Cabbage (green)/14 carrots/4 ribs celery

74. Tonsillitis
12 Carrots/2 ribs celery/handful of parsley/2 cloves garlic

75. Toxemia
12 Carrots/handful of spinach/2 cloves garlic/handful of parsley/handful of kale
And/or
12 Carrots/2 ribs celery and/or
1 pomegranate/1 inch ginger/1/2 lemon with peel

76. Tumors
12 Carrots/handful of spinach/handful of parsley/handful of kale/2 golden apples/ 5 or 6 dandelion green leaves.

77. Tuberculosis
12 Carrots/5 dandelion leaves and/or
12 Carrots/large handful of spinach

78.Worms/Parasites
12 Carrots/2 cloves of garlic/1/4 onion or
1/2 inch horseradish and/or
3 Pomegranates and/or 1 cup cranberries
with 2 golden apples

Jay's Personal Notes

Please remember, if your vegetable
juice combinations using greens taste
too strong or bitter, you may add some
golden delicious apples to sweeten the
drink. However, if you are hypoglycemic or
diabetic, please be careful with the apples.

Also, when you are juicing greens, please
juice the greens first, and then follow
through with the carrots or apples to flush
the rest of the greens out of the juicer bowl.
Please remember to use a profession juicer.

Recommended Books:

A Cancer Therapy – Dr. Max Gerson, M.D.
Rainbow Green Live food Cuisine –
Dr. Gabriel Cousins, M.D.
Fresh Vegetable Juices – Dr. Norman Walker
The Complete Book of Juicing –
Dr. Michael Murray, N.D.
The Complete Book of Enzyme Therapy–
Dr. Anthony Cichoke

w w w . j a y k o r d i c h . c o m